BUILD AND DISCOVER

ANIMALS

Written by Camilla de la Bédoyère
Illustrated by Mark Ruffle

Silver Dolphin

Silver Dolphin Books
An imprint of Printers Row Publishing Group
A division of Readerlink Distribution Services, LLC
9717 Pacific Heights Blvd, San Diego, CA 92121
www.silverdolphinbooks.com

Written by Camilla de la Bédoyère
Illustrated and designed by Mark Ruffle
Paper Engineering by Rob Ives
Commissioning Editor: William Petty
Publisher: Jonathan Gilbert

Printers Row Publishing Group is a division of Readerlink
Distribution Services, LLC.
Silver Dolphin Books is a registered trademark of Readerlink
Distribution Services, LLC.

All notations of errors or omissions should be addressed to
Silver Dolphin Books, Editorial Department, at the above address.
All other correspondence (author inquiries, permissions)
concerning the content of this book should be addressed to
Quarto Children's Books Ltd, The Old Brewery, 6 Blundell Street,
London N7 9BH UK.

ISBN: 978-1-64517-775-3
Manufactured, printed, and assembled in Shaoguan, China.
First printing, December 2021. SL/12/21
25 24 23 22 21 1 2 3 4 5

CONTENTS

MEET THE ANIMALS

Welcome to the varied and fascinating animal kingdom! Scientists have named around 1.3 million **species** of animals, and it's hard to imagine more different living things than a huge blue whale and a tiny beetle, or a simple earthworm and a clever chimpanzee. But although they are incredibly different, there are some things that all animals, including you, have in common.

INSIDE AN ANIMAL

All animals are made up of tiny basic building blocks called cells. Billions of similar cells combine together to make tissues, such as skin or bone.

ORGANS AND SYSTEMS

Tissues combine to form organs—body parts that have particular jobs to do, such as the brain or heart. Organs make up systems, such as the digestive or nervous system, which give animals what they need to stay alive.

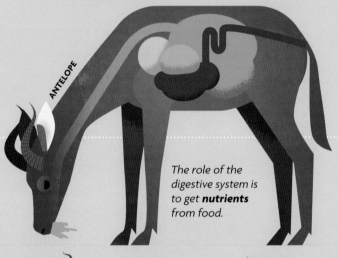

ANTELOPE

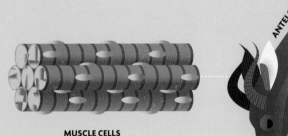

MUSCLE CELLS

*The role of the digestive system is to get **nutrients** from food.*

SEVEN THINGS ALL ANIMALS DO

Movement—can move their bodies

*Respiration—breathe in oxygen and breathe out **carbon dioxide***

Senses—take in information from the world around them

Nutrition—find and eat food

Excretion—remove waste from their bodies

Reproduction—animals produce offspring, or young

Growth—grow and change during their lives

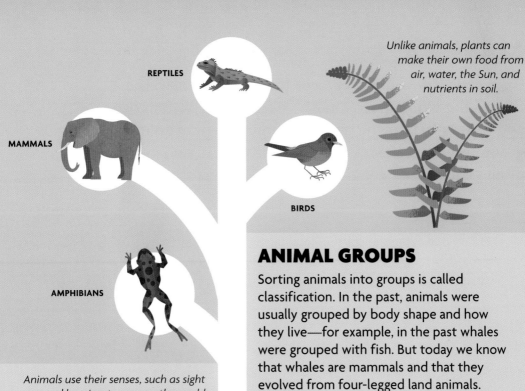

REPTILES

MAMMALS

BIRDS

Unlike animals, plants can make their own food from air, water, the Sun, and nutrients in soil.

AMPHIBIANS

ANIMAL GROUPS

Sorting animals into groups is called classification. In the past, animals were usually grouped by body shape and how they live—for example, in the past whales were grouped with fish. But today we know that whales are mammals and that they evolved from four-legged land animals.

Animals use their senses, such as sight and hearing, to process the world around them. They can use that information to move toward food or to escape from danger.

FISH

INVERTEBRATES

VERTEBRATES

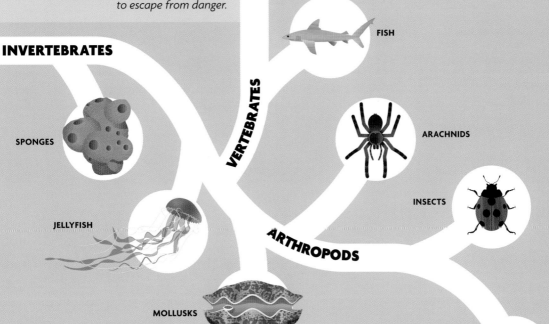

SPONGES

ARACHNIDS

INSECTS

JELLYFISH

ARTHROPODS

MOLLUSKS

CRUSTACEANS

MAMMALS

From little shrew-like creatures that lived beneath the feet of the dinosaurs, mammals have grown both in size and variety to become one of the most diverse animal groups on the planet. The biggest, strongest, and most intelligent animals are all mammals—and so are you!

WHAT MAKES A MAMMAL

These are some of the things that make mammals different from other animals.

HAIR—*mammals have hair on their bodies, although some, such as some sea mammals, only have it as babies.*

EAR BONES—*if you could see inside the ear of any mammal, you'd see three tiny bones that help transmit sound to the brain.*

SWEAT—*mammals are the only animals with sweat glands. Sweating cools the skin down, which is useful if you're furry!*

MILK—*mammals produce nutritious milk in their bodies to feed their young.*

KODIAK BEAR
At 1,500 lbs, Kodiak bears are the biggest omnivore—an animal that eats both animals and plants.

AMAZING RANGE

Mammals come in all shapes and sizes, and follow a huge range of lifestyles, from flying to swimming.

BUMBLEBEE BAT
At only 1 inch long, this tiny flying creature is the smallest mammal in the world.

STRANGE MAMMALS

Monotremes are unusual mammals that lay eggs. There are only five species of monotremes: the duck-billed platypus, the long-nosed echidna, and three species of short-nosed echidna.

MARSUPIALS

Kangaroos, koalas, and wombats are marsupials, or animals with pouches. These unusual mammals give birth to tiny babies that stay in their mother's pouch where they drink milk as they grow. Most marsupials are found in Australia.

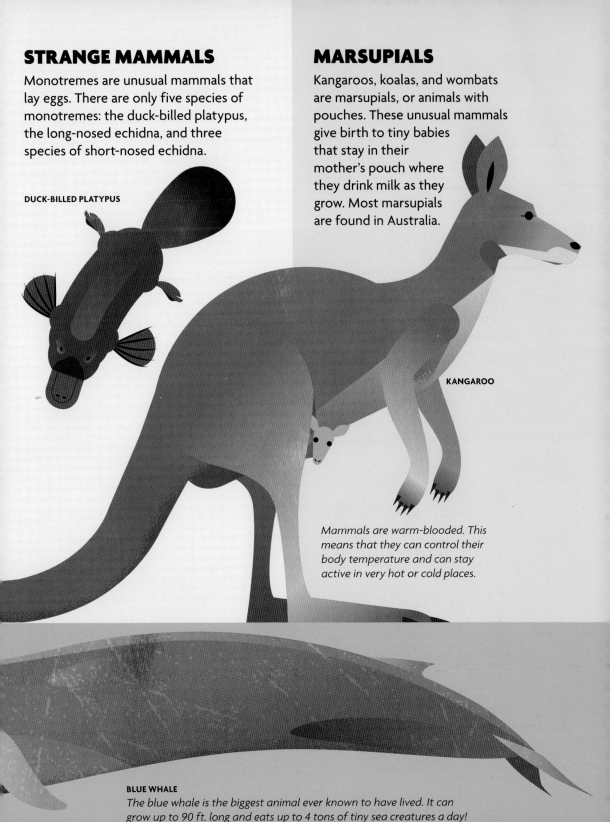

DUCK-BILLED PLATYPUS

KANGAROO

Mammals are warm-blooded. This means that they can control their body temperature and can stay active in very hot or cold places.

BLUE WHALE
The blue whale is the biggest animal ever known to have lived. It can grow up to 90 ft. long and eats up to 4 tons of tiny sea creatures a day!

BIRDS

Birds evolved from dinosaurs around 150 million years ago. Today they are found in a staggering range of shapes and sizes, from nimble flitting hummingbirds to huge soaring eagles. Thanks to their feathers, a unique body covering found only on birds, they're also some of the most colorful animals.

FLIGHT . . .

Along with bats, insects, and extinct reptiles called pterosaurs, birds are one of only four animal groups to have taken to the skies. It helps explain birds' success and variety—flying animals can escape from **predators**, travel easily in search of food, and find new homes.

With graceful wings as wide as a bus, the wandering albatross can soar for thousands of miles above the ocean in search of food.

PEREGRINE FALCON

WANDERING ALBATROSS

The fastest animal on Earth is a bird! A peregrine falcon can fly 200 mph as it dives to hunt other birds to eat.

. . . AND FLIGHTLESSNESS

Some birds have lost the power of flight and adopted new ways of life. These include ostriches and emus, which are tall two-legged sprinters, and penguins, which are awkward on land but are amazing swimmers.

The kakapo, a flightless parrot from New Zealand, lost the power of flight because there were no predators it needed to escape from. But it is now endangered due to predators introduced by humans, such as dogs and rats.

KAKAPO

SPECIAL BONES

A bird's bones are full of tiny holes. This special structure keeps the skeleton strong, but lightweight.

The wishbone acts like a spring that lifts the bird's wings.

Powerful wing muscles are attached to the breastbone.

It may look like a bird's knees bend backward, but these are its ankles—the knees are usually hidden by feathers.

FANTASTIC FEET

Most birds have three or four toes on each foot and can use their feet to perch on branches or grip food. Many birds that swim, such as ducks, have **webbing** between their toes.

THE PERFECT BEAK

The first birds had teeth, but modern birds are all toothless. The shape and size of a bird's beak is often **adapted** for the type of food it eats.

HUMMINGBIRD
*Sucks **nectar***

FINCH
Crunches seeds

TOUCAN
Reaches fruit at the tip of a branch.

REPTILES AND AMPHIBIANS

These animals are cold-blooded. Amphibians live in and around around freshwater and brackish water, water that is a little salty, but reptiles have a greater range. Some, such as sea snakes and sea turtles, live in open oceans. Some snakes and lizards are able to make their home in deserts because reptile eggs don't dry out.

SLITHERING SNAKES

Although snakes have no **limbs**, they are still speedy movers. They have long backbones, lined with many pairs of ribs and can slither on their bellies, climb, and swim.

PIT VIPER
*Snakes can't chew, but they can open their jaws wide enough to swallow their **prey** whole.*

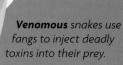

__Venomous__ snakes use fangs to inject deadly toxins into their prey.

CROCODILIANS AND LIZARDS

Members of these families usually walk on four legs and have a long tail. Most of them are predators and are equipped with keen senses for finding prey.

SALTWATER CROCODILE

The scales of a reptile are made of keratin—the same material that makes up hair, nails, and feathers.

UNUSUAL REPTILE

A tuatara looks like a lizard, but it is actually the last survivor of a different ancient group of reptiles, the rhynchocephalians. They are only found in New Zealand.

Tuataras have a third eye on the top of their heads! Scientists think it might help to detect sunlight, even though skin grows over it while they're young.

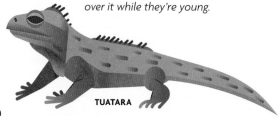

TUATARA

LIFE CYCLE

Most amphibians lay their eggs in water. They hatch into fish-like **larvae**, which breathe through gills. Gradually the larvae grow legs and lungs, and lose their gills to become adults. A transformation like this is called **metamorphosis**.

NATTERJACK TOAD

SPECIAL SKIN

The skin of an amphibian is soft and smooth. It is coated in a layer of **mucus** to keep it damp. This helps an amphibian breathe through its skin.

FROGSPAWN

The larvae of frogs and toads are called tadpoles.

Salamanders and newts keep their tails as adults, while frogs and toads lose theirs.

As adults, salamanders and newts spend more time living in water than most frogs and toads.

FROG OR TOAD?

Frogs and toads have short bodies, long legs, large mouths, and big eyes. Frogs usually have smoother skin than toads and are strong jumpers.

GREAT CRESTED NEWT

COMMON FROG

FISH

Fish were the first vertebrates—animals with a backbone—and all other vertebrates, including humans, evolved from them. So meet your distant relatives! These cold-blooded animals live in water.

BONY FISH

The largest group of fish is named for their bony skeletons. They live in salt and freshwater, and often have bodies flattened from side to side. Most have fins, but some, such as eels, have evolved a snake-like body.

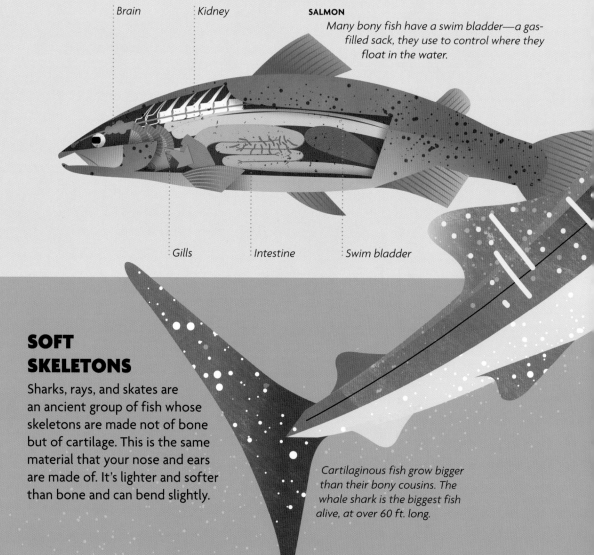

Brain

Kidney

SALMON
Many bony fish have a swim bladder—a gas-filled sack, they use to control where they float in the water.

Gills

Intestine

Swim bladder

SOFT SKELETONS

Sharks, rays, and skates are an ancient group of fish whose skeletons are made not of bone but of cartilage. This is the same material that your nose and ears are made of. It's lighter and softer than bone and can bend slightly.

Cartilaginous fish grow bigger than their bony cousins. The whale shark is the biggest fish alive, at over 60 ft. long.

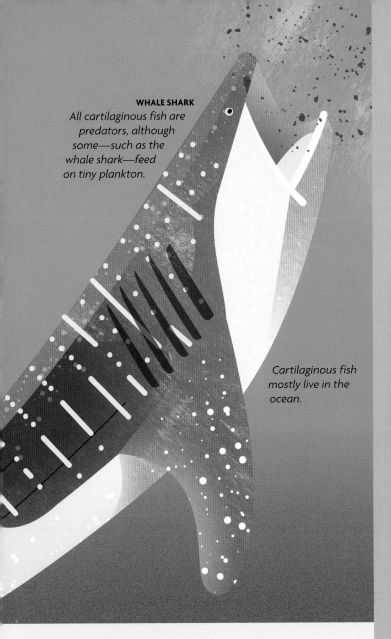

WHALE SHARK
All cartilaginous fish are predators, although some—such as the whale shark—feed on tiny plankton.

Cartilaginous fish mostly live in the ocean.

VERTEBRATES VS. INVERTEBRATES

• Vertebrates—fish, amphibians, reptiles, birds, and mammals—are named after the vertebrae, bones that make up a backbone. They have a bony internal skeleton (except for sharks and their relatives, whose skeletons are cartilage).

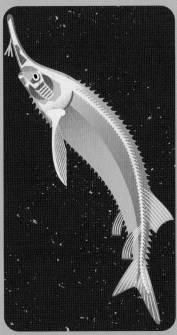

• Animals without a backbone are called invertebrates. They may have an exoskeleton (shell) or no skeleton at all.

INCREDIBLE FISH

All fish breathe in water, but there are some amazing fish that can also breathe in air. Lungfish have paddle-shaped fins that they can use to walk on the seafloor, or crawl onto land, where they hunt frogs and bugs.

AUSTRALIAN LUNGFISH

ARTHROPODS

Insects, centipedes, spiders, crabs, and shrimp are arthropods. This invertebrate group contains more than 1 million species—80 percent of all animals! They live almost everywhere on the planet, from the deep sea to the frozen poles, and although most would easily fit in your hand, some crustaceans can grow to be larger than a person.

SPIDERS AND SCORPIONS

Arachnids are arthropods with eight legs and include spiders, scorpions, harvestmen, mites, and ticks. Scorpions and most spiders inject their prey with venom to stun or kill it. Arachnids cannot chew, so after injecting venom they spit chemicals from their stomach onto their victim to dissolve the flesh before sucking up the liquid meal.

CRUSTACEANS

Crustaceans have two pairs of **antennae**, and many have strong legs for walking or swimming. The smallest crustaceans are tiny water fleas that are invisible to the naked eye, but the largest—Japanese spider crabs—can grow to be 10 ft. from tip to tip.

*The exoskeleton is toughened with **calcium carbonate**.*

The front limbs of a crab, called chelipeds, are perfect for grabbing prey or defending against predators.

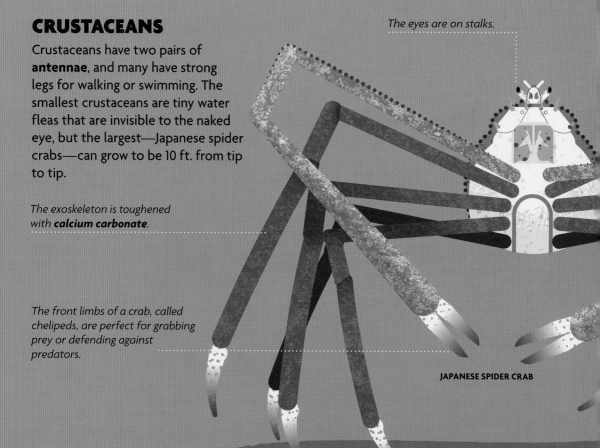

The eyes are on stalks.

JAPANESE SPIDER CRAB

Arthropod bodies are divided into two segments, and they have limbs that bend at joints.

Spiders produce silk from organs called spinnerets. They use it to build homes, trap prey in sticky webs, and swing around!

Eyes

Stomach

Intestine

Venom gland

Brain

Heart

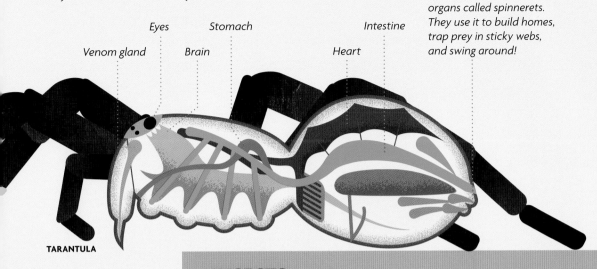

TARANTULA

INSECTS

This is the largest group of invertebrates and the only one to have evolved the power of flight. Insects have a huge range of body shapes and lifestyles, and have been able to make a home in almost every type of land habitat, as well as in water.

Crabs and other crustaceans can regrow lost legs.

An insect body has three segments: head, thorax, and abdomen.

Most adult insects have wings and can fly.

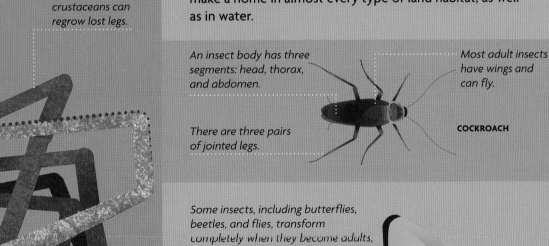

COCKROACH

There are three pairs of jointed legs.

Some insects, including butterflies, beetles, and flies, transform completely when they become adults, a process called metamorphosis. For example, a caterpillar crawls and chomps leaves, but an adult butterfly flies and can only suck up liquid.

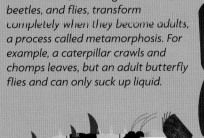

BLUE MORPHO CATERPILLAR

BLUE MORPHO BUTTERFLY

MOLLUSKS

Mollusks are a large group of invertebrates that mostly live in water, although some, such as slugs and snails, also live on land. They may have a hard shell and a muscular "foot" on their underside—this is the slimy body part that snails and slugs use to crawl on. One group, octopuses, has evolved a high level of intelligence.

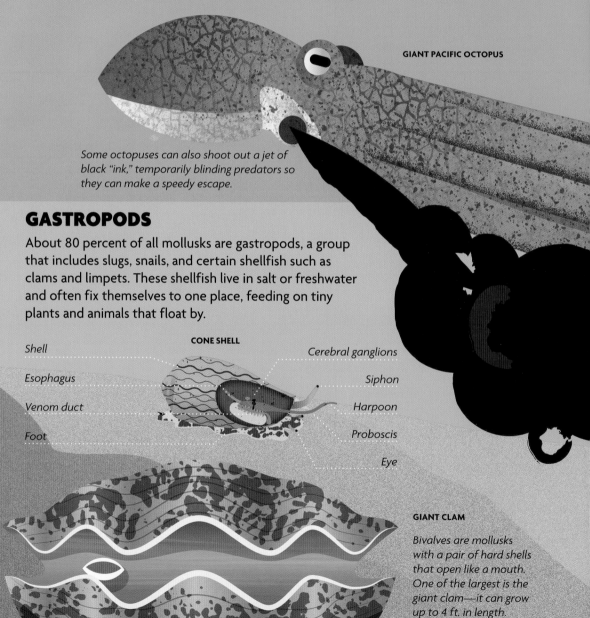

GIANT PACIFIC OCTOPUS

Some octopuses can also shoot out a jet of black "ink," temporarily blinding predators so they can make a speedy escape.

GASTROPODS

About 80 percent of all mollusks are gastropods, a group that includes slugs, snails, and certain shellfish such as clams and limpets. These shellfish live in salt or freshwater and often fix themselves to one place, feeding on tiny plants and animals that float by.

CONE SHELL

Shell

Esophagus

Venom duct

Foot

Cerebral ganglions

Siphon

Harpoon

Proboscis

Eye

GIANT CLAM

Bivalves are mollusks with a pair of hard shells that open like a mouth. One of the largest is the giant clam—it can grow up to 4 ft. in length.

MOLLUSKS ON THE MOVE

Squid, octopuses, and cuttlefish belong to a group of mollusks called cephalopods. They swim, often using a funnel that shoots out jets of water to speed through the sea. Instead of a foot, cephalopods have tentacles or arms, which they use to touch, grab, and kill prey.

SHAPE-SHIFTERS

Many cephalopods can change color and pattern, and octopuses can change their body shape, too, even mimicking other creatures such as jellyfish to avoid being attacked. Octopuses are thought to be the most intelligent invertebrates—in experiments they can solve mazes and complete puzzles for food.

An octopus has eight arms that are lined with suckers. Each sucker can fold like a pincer, so it can be used like a finger and thumb. Squid suckers are often equipped with rows of sharp "teeth" or hooks.

SEA SLUGS

Some of the most brightly colored and patterned mollusks are sea slugs, which are also known as nudibranchs. They usually live on the seafloor, and some species eat jellyfish, then absorb the jellyfish's stinging cells into their own bodies to use in defense!

This sea slug has cerata—fleshy tubes that are tipped with stinging cells. Its bright colors warn attackers to stay away.

SPONGES, WORMS, AND JELLYFISH

Worms, jellyfish, sea stars, and sponges all make up other large groups of invertebrates. Like all invertebrate groups, they first evolved in the ocean more than 500 million years ago and live there still, although one group, worms, has successfully made a home on land as well.

SIMPLE SPONGES

Sponges live in water and have the simplest bodies of all animals—unlike other animals, their cells aren't organized into tissues or organs. Sponges have an unusual skill—if a sponge's body is broken up, each part can regrow into a new animal!

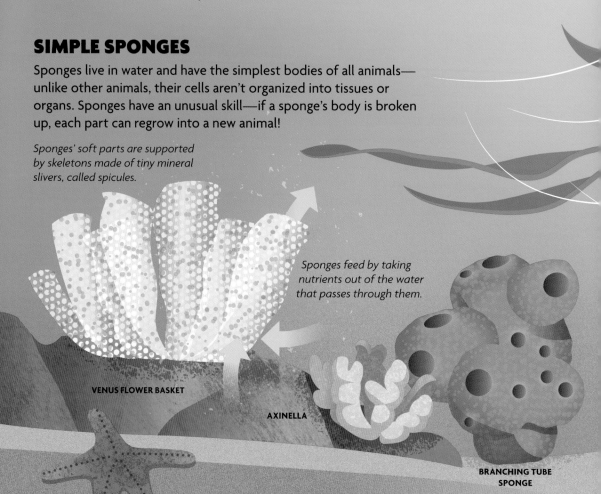

Sponges' soft parts are supported by skeletons made of tiny mineral slivers, called spicules.

Sponges feed by taking nutrients out of the water that passes through them.

VENUS FLOWER BASKET

AXINELLA

BRANCHING TUBE SPONGE

Many echinoderms have a hard skeleton made of chalky plates just under the skin that protect them from predators.

SPINY SKINS

Sea stars, sea urchins, feather stars, and sea cucumbers are all types of echinoderms, spiny-skinned invertebrates that mostly live on the seafloor. Echinoderm bodies are usually divided into five segments arranged evenly around a mouth in the center of the body.

SOFT BODIES

Jellyfish, corals, and sea anemones belong to a group called cnidarians. They have soft bodies, but tiny coral **polyps** build rocky cup-shaped structures to live in that form coral reefs many miles in length!

A ring of tentacles stings prey before moving it to the jellyfish's mouth. These animals have only one hole for food to go in and waste to go out of the body.

SEA STINGERS

Cnidarians use **tentacles** packed with stinging cells to protect themselves from attack and to stun or kill the small sea creatures they eat. Each cell contains a sharp, barbed thread that flies out like a harpoon and injects prey with toxin.

Barbed thread fired at victim ·········

Stinging cell ready to sting

FAN WORMS

WRIGGLING WORMS

Worms are soft, tube-shaped animals that live in a wide range of habitats—in water, in soil, or even inside bodies of other animals! Most worms are tiny, but the bootlace worm, which lives in the North Sea, can grow to over 100 feet long!

Fan worms are a type of worm that lives in the sea. They cling to the sea floor and filter food from the water with their fan-like tentacles.

SKELETONS

A skeleton is a framework that supports an animal's body and gives it strength. In vertebrates, that framework is inside the body, but some invertebrates have a skeleton on the outside.

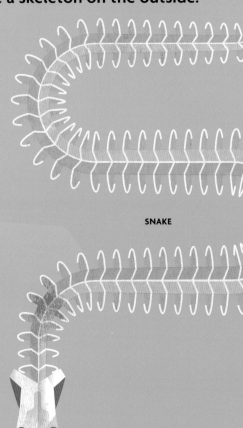

SNAKE

PIGEON

BONY SKELETONS

Bone is a hard, living tissue that is both strong and light. Most vertebrates have a bony skull to protect the brain, a backbone that bends, and four moveable limbs.

TIGER

EXOSKELETONS

The tough outer skin of an arthropod is called an exoskeleton, and it is made of a material called chitin. Chitin is sometimes compared to plastic because it is waterproof, strong, and can be colorful. It can form almost any shape and also bends slightly.

SHELLS

Most shells are made of calcium carbonate. Echinoderms and mollusks are invertebrates that often have chalky skeletons made of this mineral.

Snails are mollusks with one shell that grows bigger as the animal ages.

MUREX SHELL

Hard outer skeletons, like shells and exoskeletons, help protect an animal's internal soft body parts.

BIZARRE BONES

Over millions of years, the basic vertebrate skeleton has been adapted to suit the lives of a wide variety of animals.

ARMADILLO
An armadillo is a mammal with a bony shell. Inside the shell, it has rib, shoulder, and hip bones like other vertebrates.

FRILLED LIZARD
The strange frill on a frilled lizard's neck is supported by bones. The frill threatens predators and scares them away.

DEER
Some deer use bony antlers for fighting and attracting a mate. Antlers are shed every year and grow back bigger!

MOVING PARTS

Animals can walk, run, fly, climb, crawl, slither, or swim from one place to another to search for food and water, find shelter, or seek mates. This important skill is called locomotion.

MUSCLES

Muscles are special tissues that can stretch and **contract** to move bones or other body parts that they are attached to. A typical mammal may have as many as 600 muscles, but an insect has up to 1,800.

The bicep muscle bends the arm.

Hand muscles produce precise movements.

JOINTS

A bony skeleton is made up of many bones connected together at places called joints. Joints allow bones to move in different ways.

The tricep muscle straightens the arm

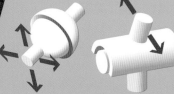

BALL & SOCKET

HINGE

GLIDING PLANE

PIVOT

ELLIPSOID

SADDLE

CHIMPANZEE

22

WATER SKELETONS

Many invertebrates use water to do the job of a skeleton, called a hydroskeleton. Water is contained in vessels, or tubes, and put under pressure by surrounding muscles to make stiff structures that can move. Sea urchins and sea stars use water-filled "tube feet" to move along the seabed.

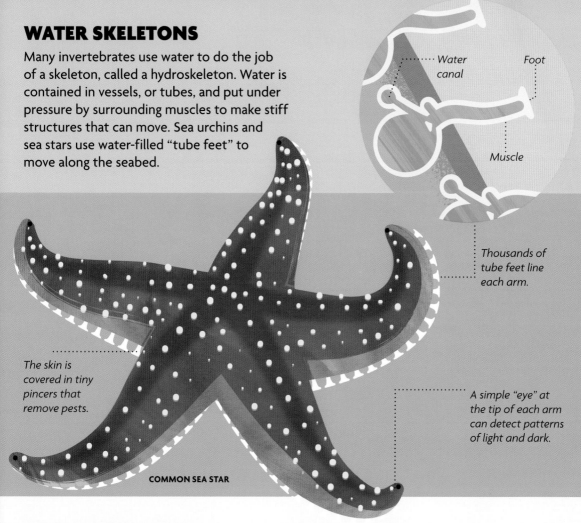

Water canal

Foot

Muscle

Thousands of tube feet line each arm.

The skin is covered in tiny pincers that remove pests.

A simple "eye" at the tip of each arm can detect patterns of light and dark.

COMMON SEA STAR

SMOOTH MOVERS

Earthworms have two sets of muscles—one set that wraps around the body and another set that runs along its length. Worms contract and relax these muscles to stretch and draw in their bodies, which allows them to travel forward.

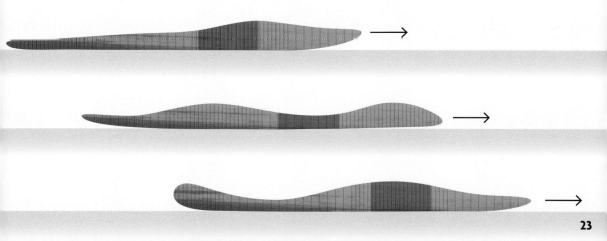

GETTING AROUND

Taking a close look at how an animal is built—its anatomy—gives useful clues about how it moves. Its skeleton, muscles, and limbs must all work together to achieve movement.

GETTING A GRIP

Animals that climb and leap need to grab hold of things as they move. Monkeys and apes have hands for gripping branches, but many smaller animals have stiff hairs on their feet that hold tight onto surfaces.

GIBBON

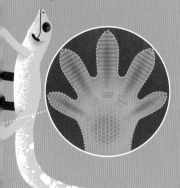

GECKO
*Some geckos uses the weak force that attracts all **molecules** to each other to defy gravity. Their feet are so densely covered in microscopic bristles that a force that's usually too small to have an effect becomes concentrated—and the geckos can walk up walls!*

Gibbons are apes that swing through the trees using their long arms and flexible hands.

BUILT FOR SPEED

Like many predators that chase their prey, a cheetah's body is built for speed. This spotted cat needs to be fast to catch antelope that graze on the African savanna where it lives. The cheetah can reach speeds of 60 miles per hour (mph) or more, but only in short bursts.

The spine is very flexible. It bends and straightens with every huge stride.

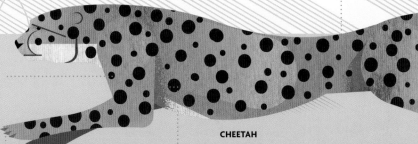

Special muscles allow the limbs to swing forward and backward.

CHEETAH

Claws grip the ground like the spikes on a runner's shoes.

The long, slender legs do not twist easily, helping prevent injury.

The tails stretches out behind the cheetah, helping it balance and change direction.

DIFFERENT FEET

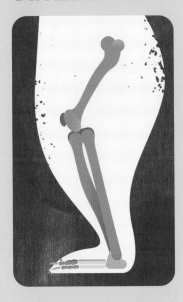

Bears and humans walk with their feet flat on the ground. This is called a plantigrade gait.

Cats and dogs walk on their toes and fingers. This is a digitigrade gait.

Horses walk on the tips of their toes, which are covered in a nail called a hoof. This is an unguligrade gait.

OUT OF THE WATER

Most fish swim by flexing their **streamlined** bodies from side to side, and use their fins to control direction. "Flying" fish use their powerful muscles to leap out of the water, and large fins are used to glide through the air!

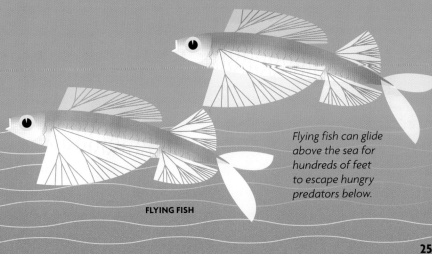

Flying fish can glide above the sea for hundreds of feet to escape hungry predators below.

FLYING FISH

AIR AND FOOD

An animal's body works like a well-oiled machine to help it live and thrive. There are important systems that allow the body to breathe oxygen, digest food, and get rid of waste.

Birds have a two-stage "circular" breathing pattern that helps them extract maximum oxygen from the air.

BREATH OF LIFE

Animals need to breathe in oxygen, a gas that is in the air or water. They use the oxygen to release energy from food, and they breathe out the waste gas—carbon dioxide—that is made during this process.

Rear stage 1: the lungs fill with air from the rear air sac.

EUROPEAN STARLING

Front stage 1: the bird breathes out, emptying the front air sac.

Front stage 2: air moves from the lungs to the front air sac.

FRONT AIR SAC

LUNGS

REAR AIR SAC

LUNGS AND GILLS

Most land vertebrates use lungs to breathe. Most fish breathe through gills, structures that filter oxygen from the water as they swim. Insects and other small animals breathe through holes in the skin called spiracles.

Mammals have a simple "tidal" breathing pattern. Lungs are dead ends that fill and empty through the same opening.

Rear stage 2: the bird breathes in, filling the rear air sac.

POWERING THE BODY

Food contains energy and nutrients, such as vitamins, that help an animal grow a healthy body. When animals eat food, their digestive system breaks it down so the nutrients can be used. Teeth, saliva, and special fluids, called enzymes, help break food up so it can be absorbed into the body and transported to the cells and tissues.

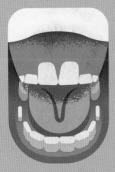

Plant eaters, such as horses, have snipping and grinding teeth.

A gharial has thin, pointy teeth for snagging slippery fish.

Chimpanzees' varied teeth reflect their omnivorous diet.

Lampreys cut a hole in their prey's skin and suck its blood!

THE DIGESTIVE SYSTEM

The digestive system begins with the mouth. As the food moves through the stomach and intestines, nutrients are removed. Waste then leaves the body at the end of the digestive system. Depending on the animal, its waste has different names, such as feces, guano, scat, dung, droppings, and excreta.

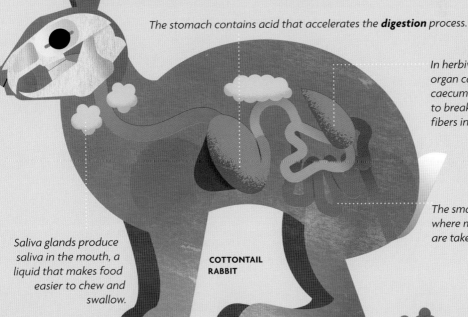

*The stomach contains acid that accelerates the **digestion** process.*

In herbivores, an organ called the caecum is enlarged to break down tough fibers in food.

The small intestine is where most nutrients are taken in.

Saliva glands produce saliva in the mouth, a liquid that makes food easier to chew and swallow.

COTTONTAIL
RABBIT

HEARTS AND BRAINS

A body's circulation system transports nutrients and oxygen, often **dissolved** in blood, to cells, tissues, and organs. The nervous system sends messages around the body and helps an animal react to changes in the world around it.

BLOOD OF LIFE

Blood is a liquid that travels around the body, carrying oxygen and nutrients, and removing waste products. Invertebrates have a blood-like fluid, called hemolymph.

PUMP

In vertebrates, blood is pumped around the body by a heart and transported in vessels called veins and arteries. In arthropods, hemolymph does not flow in vessels. Instead, it washes around the animal's insides before returning to the heart.

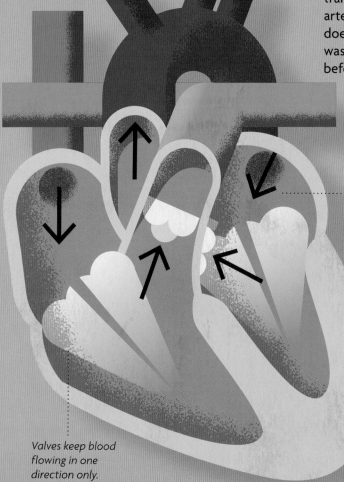

Blood carrying oxygen flows through one side of the heart. The other side pumps deoxygenated blood.

Valves keep blood flowing in one direction only.

HORMONES

A hormone is a chemical messenger that helps control the body systems, especially the systems that allow an animal to grow, change, and reproduce. Hormones usually travel in blood.

CONTROL CENTER

The brain is the body's control center. It is full of nerves that transmit information to other nerves throughout the body, creating a nervous system. Nerves are made up of cells called neurons that carry electrical signals.

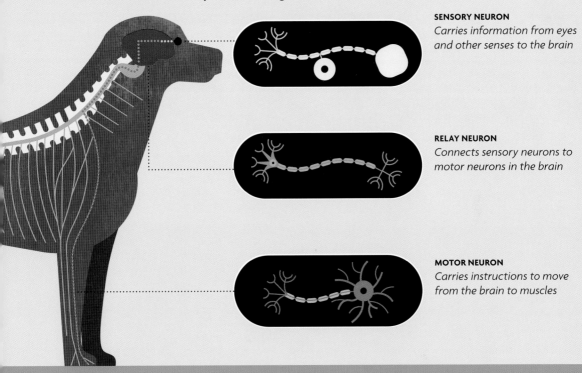

SENSORY NEURON
Carries information from eyes and other senses to the brain

RELAY NEURON
Connects sensory neurons to motor neurons in the brain

MOTOR NEURON
Carries instructions to move from the brain to muscles

INVERTEBRATES

An invertebrate's central brain is usually small and shares control with other parts of the nervous system found throughout the body.

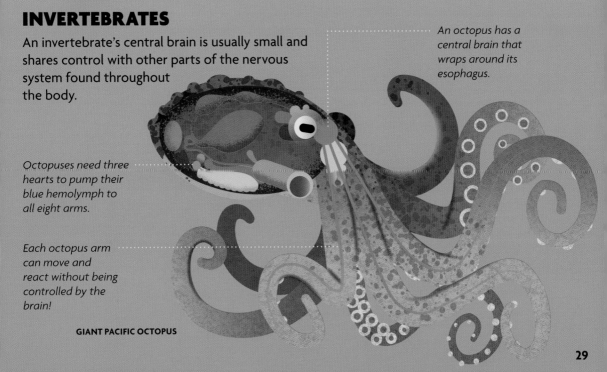

An octopus has a central brain that wraps around its esophagus.

Octopuses need three hearts to pump their blue hemolymph to all eight arms.

Each octopus arm can move and react without being controlled by the brain!

GIANT PACIFIC OCTOPUS

SENSING LIGHT AND SOUND

An animal uses its senses to find out what is happening in the world around it so it can find food and a mate, and avoid danger. Organs that can detect light and sound—eyes and ears—are some of the most important for animals' survival.

SIGHT

An eye is an organ that detects light and sends information to the brain, which turns that information into "pictures" so the animal can see. Even simple animals, such as sponges, are able to detect some light.

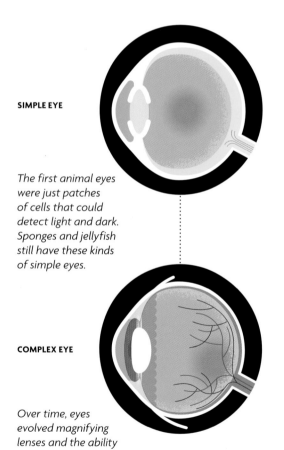

SIMPLE EYE

The first animal eyes were just patches of cells that could detect light and dark. Sponges and jellyfish still have these kinds of simple eyes.

COMPLEX EYE

Over time, eyes evolved magnifying lenses and the ability to detect millions of colors.

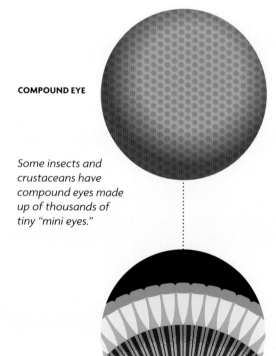

COMPOUND EYE

Some insects and crustaceans have compound eyes made up of thousands of tiny "mini eyes."

Compound eyes give wide vision and can detect very fast movement—handy for flying animals such as dragonflies.

HEARING

Ears detect sound and are the main organs for hearing. Many animals, such as cats, dogs, bats, and dolphins, are able to hear sounds that are impossible for humans to hear.

A fennec fox's big ears act like a satellite dish, focusing sound into the ear canal.

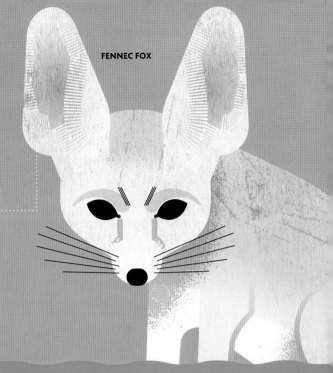

FENNEC FOX

ECHOLOCATION

Bats and some members of the whale family, such as dolphins, are able to use sound to find objects. They make sounds that bounce off solid objects and back to their ears. These echoes tell the animal about the size, shape, and position of an object.

An organ in a dolphin's head called the melon helps direct sound waves into the water.

BOTTLENOSE DOLPHIN

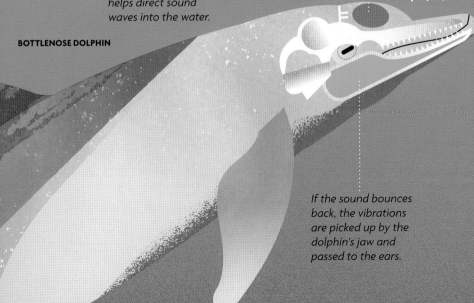

If the sound bounces back, the vibrations are picked up by the dolphin's jaw and passed to the ears.

OTHER SENSES

Just like us, animals can detect chemicals while smelling and tasting. And they detect pressure—the sense of touch. Some creatures benefit from extra senses, such as an electro-sense. There may be many more animal senses that we do not know about yet.

TASTE

Vertebrate tongues are covered in **receptors** called taste buds. They detect different chemicals in food and identify whether it's good to eat or is poisonous.

SMELL

When an animal smells something, it is detecting tiny particles of chemicals that are carried in the air or water. A good sense of smell not only helps an animal detect danger before it gets too close, but is often an essential sense for finding food.

Snakes flick their tongues to direct scents into their mouths where the scents can be tasted.

Some snakes use body parts called pit organs to detect other animals' body heat.

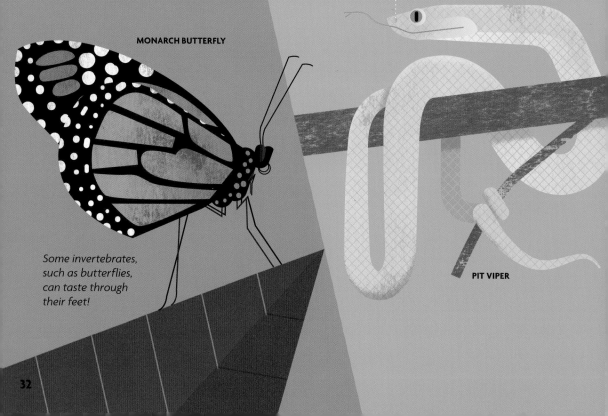

MONARCH BUTTERFLY

Some invertebrates, such as butterflies, can taste through their feet!

PIT VIPER

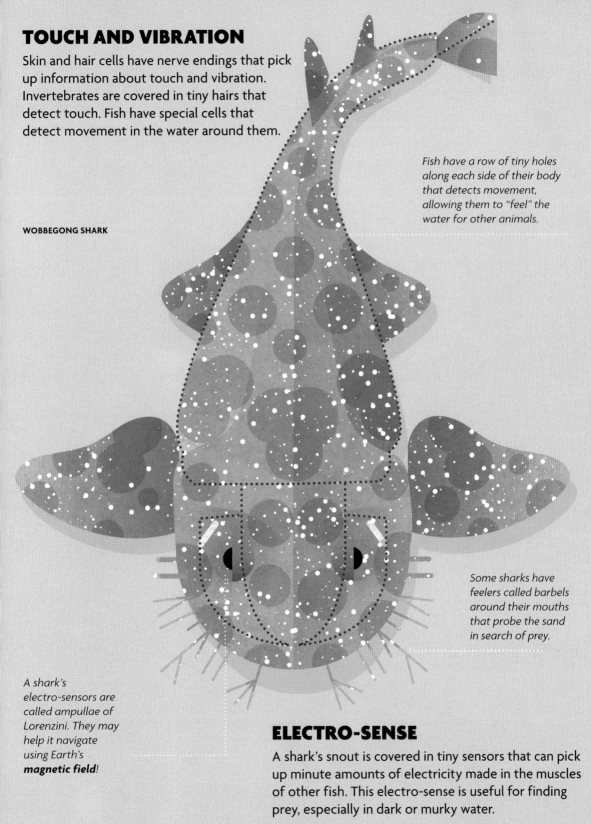

TOUCH AND VIBRATION

Skin and hair cells have nerve endings that pick up information about touch and vibration. Invertebrates are covered in tiny hairs that detect touch. Fish have special cells that detect movement in the water around them.

WOBBEGONG SHARK

Fish have a row of tiny holes along each side of their body that detects movement, allowing them to "feel" the water for other animals.

Some sharks have feelers called barbels around their mouths that probe the sand in search of prey.

*A shark's electro-sensors are called ampullae of Lorenzini. They may help it navigate using Earth's **magnetic field**!*

ELECTRO-SENSE

A shark's snout is covered in tiny sensors that can pick up minute amounts of electricity made in the muscles of other fish. This electro-sense is useful for finding prey, especially in dark or murky water.

SKIN, SCALES, AND FUR

An animal's body is protected by a shell, skin, scales, hair, or an exoskeleton. These body coverings keep the inside organs and tissues safe and give an animal color, patterns, and shape. They can also detect important information, such as touch and temperature.

SKIN

Skin can make mucus, produce sweat to help a vertebrate cool down, and store fat to keep an animal warm. Hair, scales, and feathers grow out of the skin. The skin of many soft-bodied invertebrates is much more than a covering—it also works as an organ for breathing and removing waste.

POISON ARROW FROG

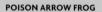

Just touching the brightly colored skin of a poison frog can be deadly!

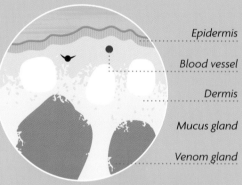

Epidermis

Blood vessel

Dermis

Mucus gland

Venom gland

HAIR AND SCALES

Furry mammals are able to grow hair from their skin. Fur keeps an animal warm, and stiff hairs, such as bristles, form whiskers that are very sensitive to touch. Fish and reptiles grow hard scales from their skin, which gives them extra protection.

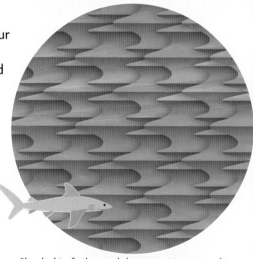

A tiger's striped fur helps it camouflage in a wide range of habitats.

Shark skin feels rough because it's covered in millions of tiny scales called dermal denticles.

FEATHERS

Birds have two main types of feathers. Soft, downy feathers keep a bird warm, and flight feathers are mostly long and stiff, and give a bird a streamlined shape when it flies. A bird uses its flight feathers to control the flow of air over its wings and tail so it can fly.

BIRD-OF-PARADISE

COLORFUL BODIES

Animals use color to hide, to draw attention to themselves, and to communicate with each other. Male birds-of-paradise use vibrant displays of colorful feathers to impress females at mating time.

A ring-tailed lemur waves its striped tail to signal to other members of its group.

RING-TAILED LEMUR

HERBIVORES

Plants take the Sun's energy and turn it into sugars, which they store in their leaves, seeds, fruits, roots, and stems. This means plants are a good source of food for animals—plants are easy to find and cannot run away! However, plants can be difficult to digest.

AFRICAN ELEPHANT

TOUGH PLANTS

Leaves and stems are tough to eat. Many herbivores have strong jaws and teeth that grind and mash plant material before it reaches the stomach. Others prefer to eat softer, juicier parts such as fruits and flowers.

CHEWING THE CUD

Cattle, deer, antelope, sheep, and giraffes feed on plants, especially grass. They are known as ruminants and have four chambers in their stomach. Food is chewed and swallowed once, then brought up back into the mouth to be chewed again!

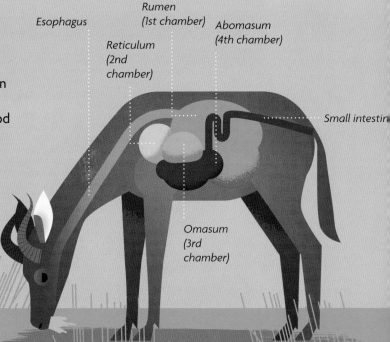

Esophagus

Rumen
(1st chamber)

Reticulum
(2nd chamber)

Abomasum
(4th chamber)

Small intestine

Omasum
(3rd chamber)

ANTELOPE

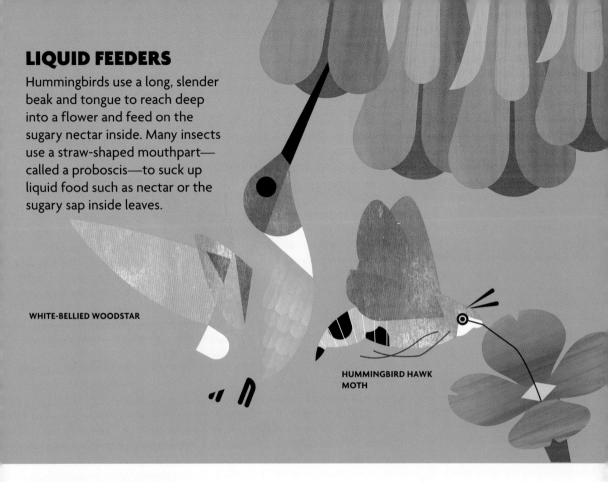

LIQUID FEEDERS

Hummingbirds use a long, slender beak and tongue to reach deep into a flower and feed on the sugary nectar inside. Many insects use a straw-shaped mouthpart—called a proboscis—to suck up liquid food such as nectar or the sugary sap inside leaves.

WHITE-BELLIED WOODSTAR

HUMMINGBIRD HAWK MOTH

FLEXIBLE FEEDERS

Kinkajous are omnivores from rain forests in South and Central America. They use their nimble hands to pick fruits and a long tongue to lap up flower nectar or honey from beehives. Kinkajous also eat insects, especially ants.

KINKAJOU

HUNTING FOR FOOD

Finding and killing other animals to eat can be a difficult and dangerous task. However, predators are rewarded with protein-packed meals that can be much easier to digest than a plant-based diet.

BALD EAGLE

CUNNING CARNIVORES

Predators may need deadly weapons and other skills, such as speed or superb senses, to be successful hunters. Members of the cat family are carnivores with sharp teeth and claws for gripping, cutting, and stabbing, while birds of prey are equipped with **talons**, incredible eyesight, and powerful beaks.

JAGUAR

Jaguars sneak up on their prey while staying hidden, then pounce when they are close. They have the most powerful bite of any big cat!

STINGS AND VENOM

Injecting venom, with stings or spines, is a fast way to overpower a dangerous target. Spiders inject venom with fangs, while centipedes use special claws. Coneshells fire a venomous dart at their victim, and many snakes and some lizards have a venomous bite.

Komodo dragons are giant lizards. Their powerful bite is also venomous, so even if a victim escapes an attack, it won't get far.

KOMODO DRAGON

AMBUSH!

Many predators save energy by sitting and waiting for their prey to pass by. Crocodiles lurk in the water, ready to ambush animals that come to drink at the water's edge. Powerful jaws, lined with sharp teeth, are all the weapons these predators need.

CROCODILE

UNUSUAL FEEDERS

Finding enough food to eat is a constant battle for most animals. These creatures have discovered that following an unusual diet means they do not have to compete with many other animals for food.

SCAVENGERS

Rotting plant matter and animal flesh do not make a tempting meal for most creatures but can still contain plenty of nutrients.

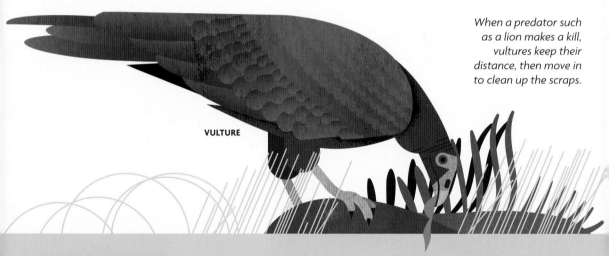

When a predator such as a lion makes a kill, vultures keep their distance, then move in to clean up the scraps.

VULTURE

DUNG EATERS

Even animal dung has useful nutrients that some creatures can use. Some dung beetles collect the dung of large mammals, such as elephants. They roll it into balls and lay their eggs inside the dung. When the larvae hatch, they eat the dung.

DUNG BEETLE

*By burying dung, dung beetles **fertilize** the soil, and spread seeds so plants can grow.*

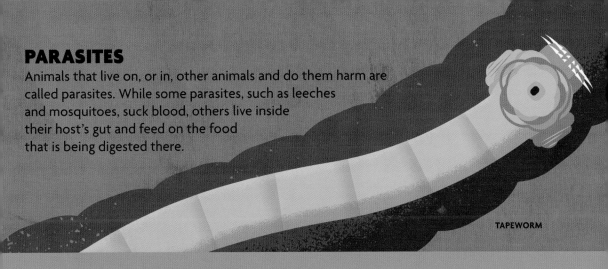

PARASITES

Animals that live on, or in, other animals and do them harm are called parasites. While some parasites, such as leeches and mosquitoes, suck blood, others live inside their host's gut and feed on the food that is being digested there.

TAPEWORM

BLOOD-SUCKING BATS

Most bats feed on flying insects or fruit, but vampire bats live entirely on a diet of blood. They have a superb sense of smell that helps them find their hosts—often cattle or horses. They use their razor-sharp teeth for gently slicing through their prey's skin.

VAMPIRE BAT

A vampire bat laps up blood that oozes from a wound. Its saliva has special chemicals that keep the blood flowing.

DEFENSE

The key to staying alive is not just finding food to eat—it is just as important to avoid being eaten! Animals have many ways to keep predators away, from prickly spines to venomous stings and clever camouflage.

WARNING SIGNS

One of the best survival tricks is to scare predators away before they get dangerously close. Animals often make themselves appear bigger and show their weapons—horns, teeth, and claws.

Sun bitterns spread their wings to scare predators away. The colorful pattern on the wings look like two enormous eyes!

SUN BITTERN

TOXIC TERRORS

Most animals with poisonous skin, venomous bites, or stings show predators that they are equipped with lethal weapons. Bright colors and stripes make good warning signs.

Sharks, eels, and other predators might try to eat a lionfish—but they'd get a toxic shock!

Thirteen sharp and venomous spines on the back

As the sharp spine is injected into an attacker, the colorful skin slips down so the spine can move smoothly into the flesh. The spine releases venom and causes great pain—and can even kill.

Bold pattern of stripes acts as a warning to predators

More venomous spines on the fins

LIONFISH

FIGHT TO SURVIVE

When an animal is under attack, it must decide to flee or fight—but it's not always possible to avoid a brutal battle. Gemsbok antelopes can run fast, but if they can't escape, they will put up a tough fight.

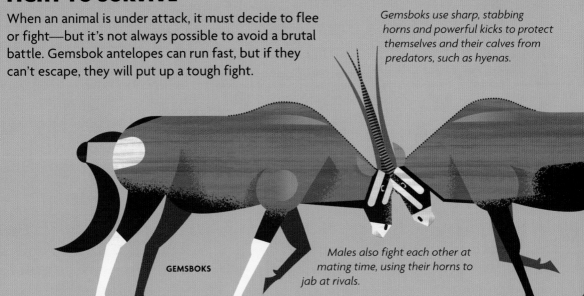

Gemsboks use sharp, stabbing horns and powerful kicks to protect themselves and their calves from predators, such as hyenas.

GEMSBOKS

Males also fight each other at mating time, using their horns to jab at rivals.

TOP TRICKS

Staying out of sight is a good way for an animal to defend itself. Camouflage, using color, pattern, or body shape, can help prey stay hidden.

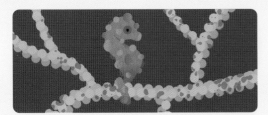

Pygmy seahorses are tiny fish with perfect camouflage that matches their coral habitat in warm, shallow seas. The skin is colored and bumpy to match the coral.

Leafy sea dragons are masters of disguise. They need camouflage because they have no other way to defend themselves. This fish's body looks like strands of seaweed that drift in the water.

With twig-like brown or green bodies, walking sticks blend perfectly in to the habitats where they live. They stay still for hours at a time, and some can change color.

A leaf insect's wings are so well camouflaged that they even have the pattern of "veins" seen on a real leaf. It copies, or mimics, the size, shape, and color of a leaf so it can feed in safety.

MAKING A HOME

A home is a safe place to shelter and look after young. Some animal architects construct their own homes. They may dig a burrow, build a nest or—in some cases—work together to change whole landscapes to suit them!

BIRD HOMES

Birds are among the animal kingdom's most skilled builders. They make nests from leaves, mud, twigs, and soft plant matter—whatever materials they can find!

AMERICAN ROBIN

Many nests are cup-shaped so the eggs and chicks don't fall out.

HOUSE MARTIN

House martins build nests from mud stuck to the sides of buildings or under roofs.

WEAVING A NEST

Male weaver birds build nests from grass, using knots to knit the blades of grass together. Some of these nests have tunnels at the entrance, making it harder for snakes to steal the eggs inside.

WEAVER BIRD

Once a male has built his nest, he hangs upside down and flaps his wings to show his mate that the nest is ready.

BUSY BEAVERS

Beavers first create a pond of deep water by building a dam made of trunks and branches they have cut with their strong teeth. Then the beavers add more wood to create an artificial island called a lodge, with underwater tunnels and dry chambers inside.

*The teeth of **rodents**, such as beavers, grow throughout their lives, so they never get worn down by all the chewing.*

DAM

LODGE

POND

Beavers' dams change the landscape, creating a habitat for many other animals.

ENTRANCE

Beavers reach the lodge using underwater entrances. This makes it difficult for predators to reach the family.

A beaver's teeth are orange because they are strengthened with iron.

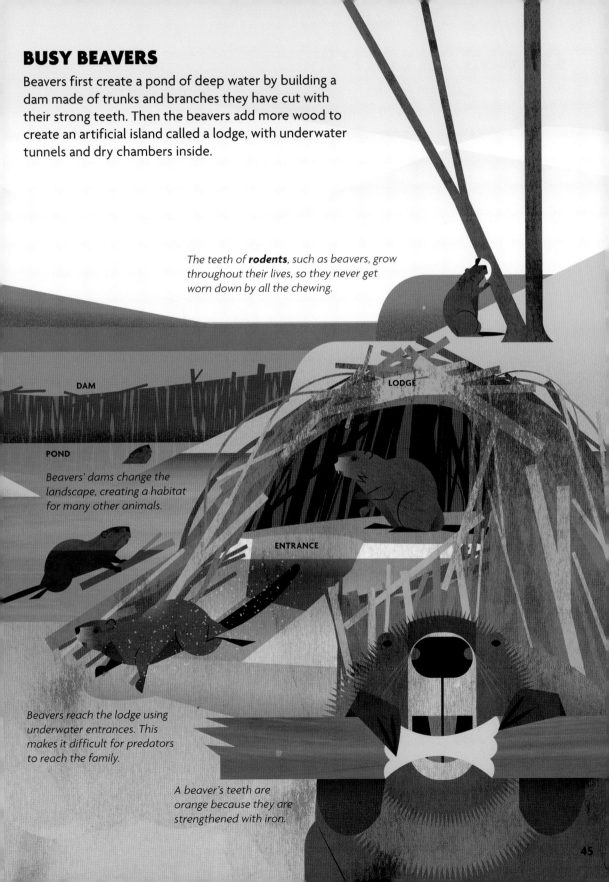

COMMUNICATION

Animals may not use words, but they can still communicate with each other. They use many different types of communication from song and dance to smell and color.

BODY LANGUAGE

Wolves, like many other animals, use their whole bodies to communicate. They snarl and show their teeth to scare other members of the pack, who cower and lie down in reply. Chimps have very expressive faces and can use them to show fear and anger, or when they want to play.

GRAY WOLF

Hoot—excited

Bulging lips—angry

Scream—nervous or excited

Full toothed smile—afraid

Pout—affectionate

Covered upper lip—playful

CHIMPANZEE

SONG AND DANCE

Like us, animals can use sounds to talk to each other. Birds are some of the most vocal animals, and male birds often dance, too. Male bullfrogs have a booming mating call that can be heard over half a mile away.

A male bullfrog puffs up a pouch in its throat that acts like an amplifier for its mating call.

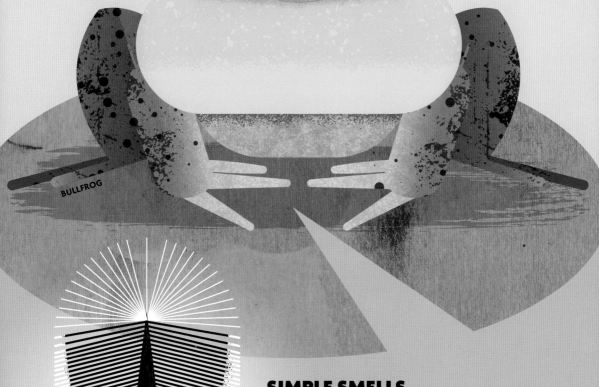

BULLFROG

SKUNK

SIMPLE SMELLS

One of the simplest ways to communicate is using smell. Invertebrates use smelly chemicals called pheromones to attract each other at mating time. Vertebrates often mark their territories using smells that warn other animals to stay away.

Skunks drive off predators by squirting a terrible-smelling liquid from their bottoms. Sometimes they do a handstand to get a better aim!

47

LAYING EGGS

All animals reproduce—this means they produce offspring, or young. Most offspring come from two parents and begin their lives as eggs that grow inside a mother's body. Some offspring are kept inside the mother's body as they develop, but most animals lay their eggs.

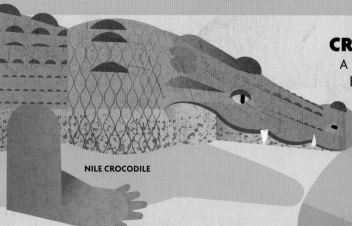

NILE CROCODILE

CROCODILE EGGS

A Nile crocodile lays up to sixty eggs in a hole she has dug on a sandy riverbank. She covers them with more sand and grass to hide them from predators. The mother protects her nest night and day.

A SAFE PLACE

An egg is a safe place for the baby crocodile to grow, which takes about eighty-five days. It is called an embryo at this stage. Inside the egg is an egg yolk, which provides energy for the embryo to grow. The egg white, or albumen, contains water and protein.

The eggshell is tough and strong to protect the growing baby inside. Air can pass through the eggshell so the young animal can breathe.

Yolk

Embryo

Albumen

CROCODILE EGG

THE EGG TOOTH

When they are ready to hatch, young crocodiles call out to their mother. Each one has a strong spike at the tip of its snout called an egg tooth. They use this spike to break out of the egg, but if they need help, their mother gently picks up the egg in her mouth and squeezes it to free the baby.

Egg tooth

YOUNG CROCODILE HATCHING

READY TO SWIM

The mother carries her newly hatched babies to the water. They may be small, but they are ready to swim and start looking for food. She protects them from predators while they grow big enough to look after themselves.

Despite having the strongest bite of any animal, a mother Nile crocodile gently carries her babies in her mouth without harming them.

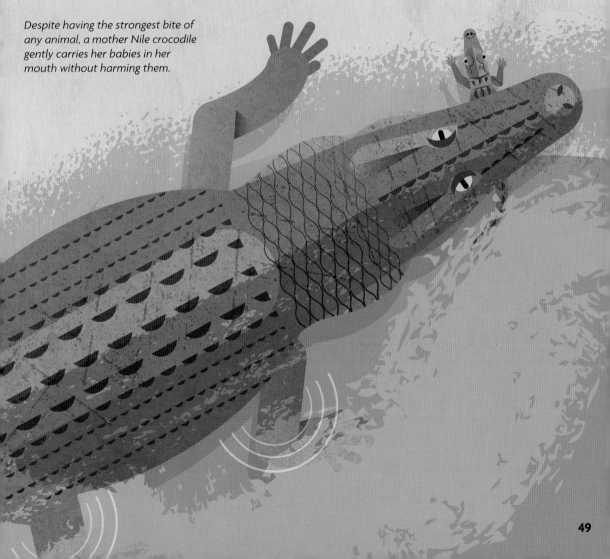

FAMILY LIFE

Most mammals keep their young inside their bodies while they develop and then give birth to them. Their young are often weak and helpless, and need their parents to take care of them—sometimes for years.

ELEPHANT CALF

The time when a baby is growing inside its mother is called a pregnancy. An African elephant is pregnant for two years while its baby, or calf, grows in her uterus. Nutrients the baby needs from the mother pass through a body part called the placenta, which also removes waste.

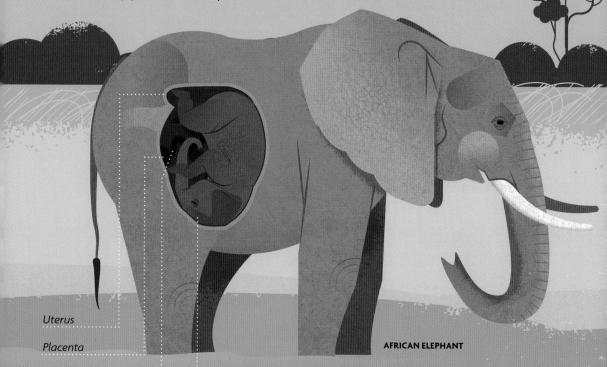

Uterus

Placenta

Umbilical cord

Developing baby elephant

AFRICAN ELEPHANT

BIG FAMILIES

An elephant usually has just one calf at a time and does not get pregnant again for up to five years. Smaller mammals, however, often have big litters. Some shrews have up to six babies in each litter and up to five litters every year. One European rabbit can give birth to 360 babies in her lifetime!

FAMILY LIFE

When the elephant calf is born, it can feed on its mother's milk, but other members of the family will help raise it. They all come and greet the newborn, stroking it with their trunks. The whole family works together to protect the young calves and teach them how to find food and water.

An elephant family is called a herd and is led by an older female, who is often a grandmother. Aunts, cousins, and siblings all help the new mother.

TIME TO LEARN

Many young animals stay with their parents so they are more likely to survive. This is a time of learning and practicing essential life skills, such as hunting and hiding from predators.

EVOLUTION AND EXTINCTION

Earth is around 4.5 billion years old, but the oldest animal fossils are only around 540 million years old. Since then, animals have changed from small and simple sea creatures to the large range alive today.

Birds evolved from dinosaurs about 150 million years ago. Archaeopteryx was one of the first birds. Unlike today's birds, it had teeth, claws, and a bony tail.

WHAT IS EVOLUTION?

Evolution is the way that animals and plants change over time. Evolving makes them more likely to survive in an ever-changing world. Most evolution happens very slowly, but scientists learn about it by studying **fossils**.

ARCHAEOPTERYX

NATURAL SELECTION

For wild animals, every day is a battle for food, water, and mates. They compete with each other for these precious resources, and the winners are more likely to reproduce. This is called natural selection. Animals that do not adapt become extinct.

Tiktaalik was a fish that lived 375 million years ago. Like modern lungfish, it used its leg-like fins to walk on land. Fish like this evolved to become tetrapods—vertebrates with four limbs that live on land.

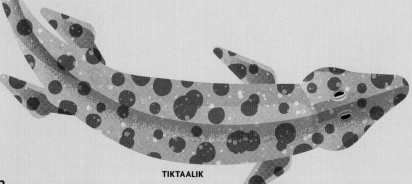

TIKTAALIK

WIPEOUT

Sometimes, enormous changes affect Earth and make it difficult for many living things to survive. Huge numbers are wiped out. These are called mass extinction events, when up to 90 percent of all animal and plant species go extinct.

*Around 66 million years ago, a giant **asteroid** smashed into the planet, altering the climate. This wiped out dinosaurs, some marine reptiles, and pterosaurs.*

CONSERVATION

Scientists believe extinctions are now happening much faster than normal, probably due to humans altering, destroying, and polluting animals' habitats. These are some practical steps you can to take to help protect animals.

Avoid disposable plastic items such as cups and plates as they end up in the oceans and harm sealife.

Farming is the biggest cause of habitat destruction, so try to cut down on meat, especially beef.

Support an animal conservation charity through fundraising and telling people about their work.

INSTRUCTIONS

On the following pages, you will find the instructions
for building your animal models. Carefully push out
the pieces from the card sheets before you begin.
If the parts don't fit together easily, widen the slots
slightly with the tip of a pen.

ELEPHANT

With raising head

Use a one-armed
motor from your kit.

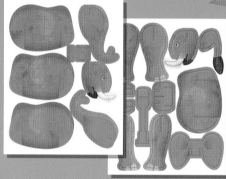

Turn to pages 58–59.

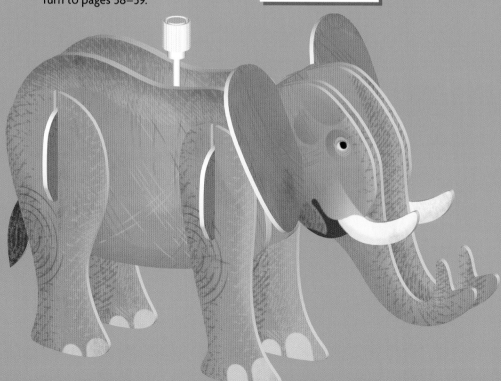

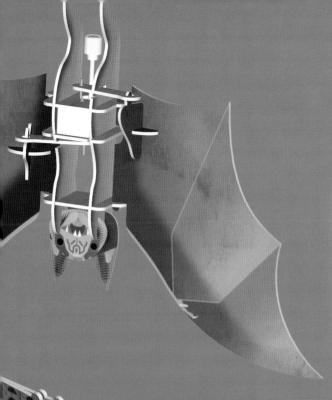

BAT
With flapping wings

Use a two-armed motor from your kit.

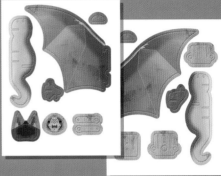

Turn to pages 56–57.

CROCODILE
With snapping jaws

Use a one-armed motor from your kit.

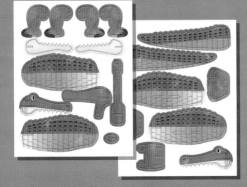

Turn to pages 60-61.

BAT

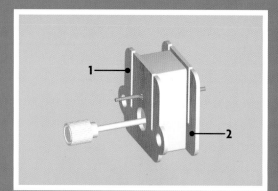

1. Line up the rear wing holder (1) and the motor holder (2) with the motor, with the winder passing through the large hole.

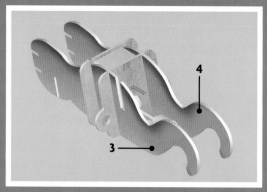

2. Slide the left body side (3) and right body side (4) onto the motor holders, with the winder toward the feet.

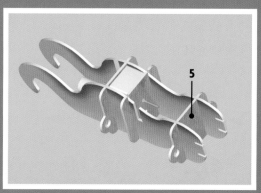

3. Slide the front wing holder (5) into the body sides.

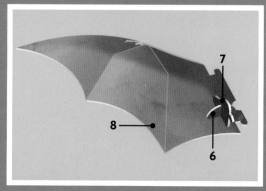

4. Slot the left wing linkage base (6) into the left wing linkage (7), and the left wing linkage into the left wing (8). Slide to lock.

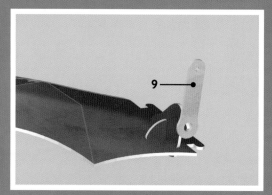

5. Using a pen, widen the large hole in the left push rod (9) until it slides onto the left wing linkage without forcing and turns freely.

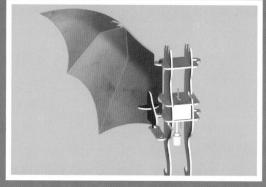

6. Fit the left wing into the holes in the wing holders. You may have to bend the wing holders slightly.

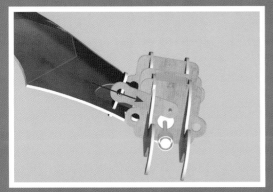

7. Slide the end of the left push rod through the slot in the body, and carefully thread the small hole onto the motor arm.

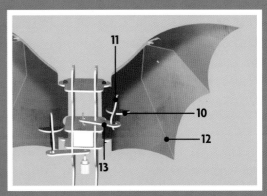

8. Repeat steps 4–7 to construct the right wing (10–13).

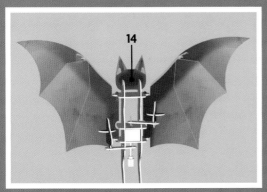

9. Slide the head (14) into the body sides.

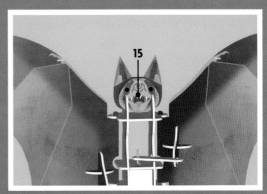

10. Slide the face (15) into the body sides to complete the model.

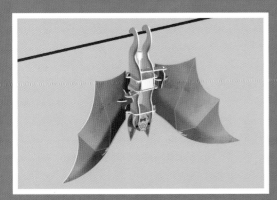

11. The bat will hang upside down by its feet if you hook it over a washing line or string hung between two objects.

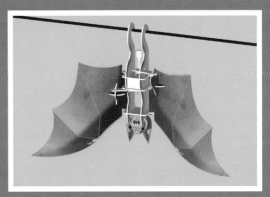

12. Wind up the motor and release to see the bat flap its wings.

ELEPHANT

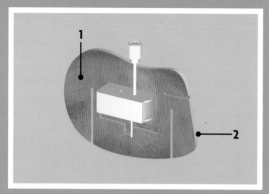

1. Push the motor into the hole in the left inner side (1) with the winder at the front, and position the left outer side (2) so that the slots line up.

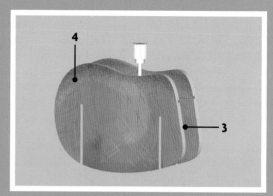

2. Position the right inner side (3) and right outer side (4) so that the motor is held in place.

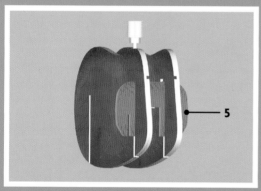

3. Holding the sides so the motor doesn't fall out, slide the shoulder plate (5) onto the body sides.

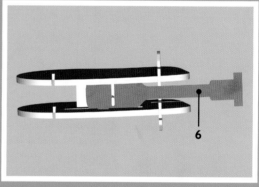

4. Fit the push rod (6) into the body so that the slot fits over the motor arm and the narrow part fits through the gap in the shoulder plate.

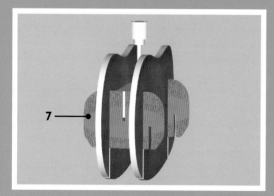

5. Slide the hip plate (7) onto the body sides to lock the body.

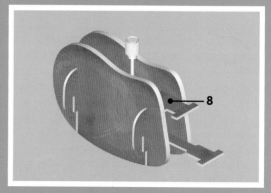

6. Slide the head pivot (8) into the slots in the front of the inner sides.

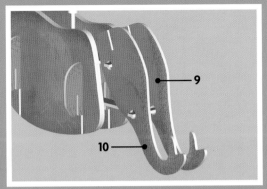

7. Fit the inner head sides (9 & 10) onto the push rod and head pivot, widening the holes with a pen if needed so the head can move freely.

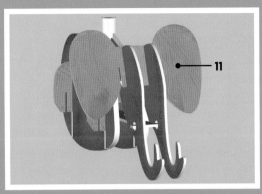

8. Slide the inner slots in the ears (11) onto the top of the inner head sides.

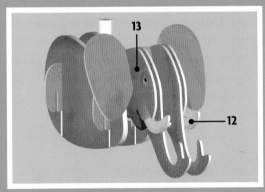

9. Slide the outer head sides (12 & 13) into the outer slots in the ears.

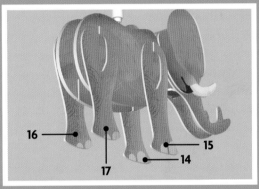

10. Slide the front legs (14 & 15) into the shoulder plate and the rear legs (16 & 17) into the hip plate.

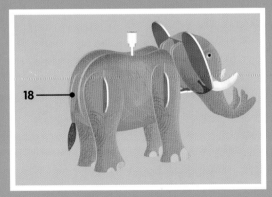

11. Slide the tail (18) into the hip plate to complete the model.

12. Wind up the motor and release to see the elephant move its head.

CROCODILE

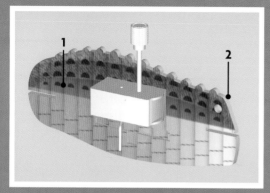

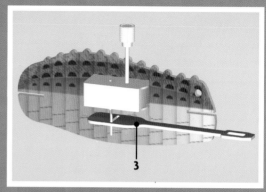

1. Push the motor into the hole in the left inner side (1) with the winder at the front, and position the left outer side (2) so that the slots line up.

2. Thread the push rod (3) over the motor arm so its edge lies in the slot in the left inner side.

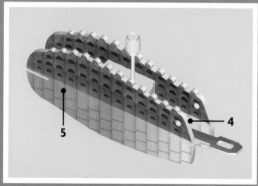

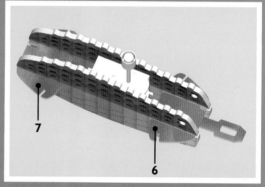

3. Position the right inner side (4) and right outer side (5) so that the motor and push rod are held in place.

4. Holding the sides so the motor and push rod don't fall out, slide the shoulder plate (6) and hip plate (7) onto the body sides to lock the body.

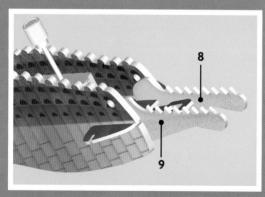

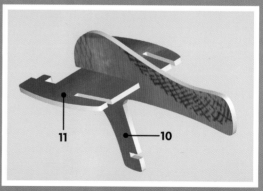

5. Slide the lower jaws (8 & 9) onto the shoulder plate.

6. Slide the jaw lifter (10) onto the head plate (11).

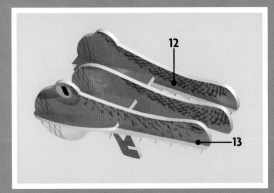

7. Slide the upper jaws (12 & 13) onto the head plate.

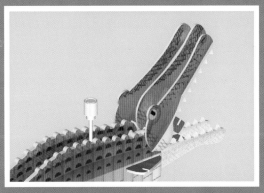

8. Attach the head plate to the body sides, widening the holes with a pen if needed so the head can move freely.

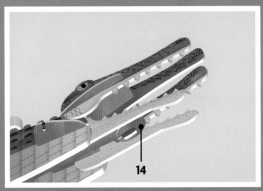

9. Push the bottom of the jaw lifter through the slot in the push rod, and slide the jaw lifter lock (14) onto the jaw lifter to secure it.

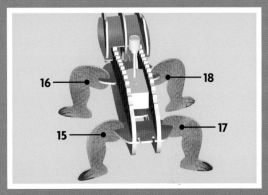

10. Slide the legs (15–18) into the hip and shoulder plates.

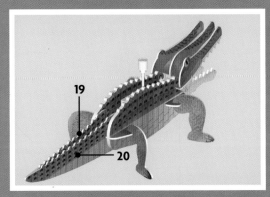

11. Slide the tail sides (19 & 20) into the hip plate to complete the model.

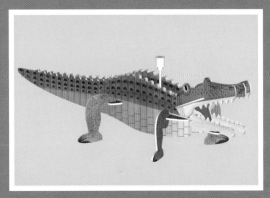

12. Wind up the motor and release to see the crocodile open and close its jaws.

GLOSSARY

ADAPTED
Changed or adjusted for a new use or situation

ANTENNAE
Long, thin structures on some invertebrates' heads, used for sensing their surroundings

ASTEROID
A small rocky body that orbits the Sun; they are sometimes called minor planets

CALCIUM CARBONATE
A mineral found in chalk and other rocks

CARBON DIOXIDE
A gas that animals breathe out as a waste product, and plants take in

CONTRACT
Get smaller and draw closer together

DIGESTION
Process where animals break down food inside their bodies and take in nutrients

DISSOLVED
Broken down and mixed with a liquid

FERTILIZE
Make soil more productive by adding substances that plants need to grow

FOSSILS
Impressions of long-dead living things that have been preserved in rock

LARVAE
First stage of an insect or amphibian's life cycle after it hatches, usually looking very different from the adult

LIMBS
Jointed structures that animals use to get around, such as arms or legs

MAGNETIC FIELD
An invisible shell surrounding an object made up of magnetic forces

METAMORPHOSIS
A total transformation of body shape between life stages

MOLECULES
A group of two or more atoms, the tiny building blocks of the universe, held together by electric forces

MUCUS
A slimy substance produced by animals' bodies to keep moist

NECTAR
A sugary liquid made by flowers

NUTRIENTS
Chemicals that living things need to survive and grow

POLYPS
A stage in the life cycle of cnidarians, where the animal attaches itself to rock or other polyps and feeds with tentacles

PREDATORS
Animals that hunt other animals for food

PREY
An animal that is hunted by other animals for food

RECEPTORS
Body parts that recognize something happening and send a message about it to the brain

RODENTS
A group of mammals with large teeth for chewing tough materials

SPECIES
A group of individual living things that have similar characteristics and can breed with each other

STREAMLINED
Shaped for cutting through water or air

TALONS
Claws of a bird of prey

TENTACLES
Long, flexible body parts that some invertebrates use for sensing and grasping

VENOMOUS
Producing a toxin that is injected into victims

WEBBING
Flexible tissue that stretches between solid parts